D1118908

WITHDRAWN
FROM
COLLECTION

'Fascinating! On the one hand this book describes a journey into London through the eyes of a young man with autism, but beneath the surface is a voyage of self-discovery as Michael addresses his autism head on and finds his place in the world. Highly recommended.'

— Jerry Hughes, CEO, Burgess Autistic Trust

'This book is easy to read, with lots of pictures. It offers an insight into the thought processes of a person on the spectrum, which many others will be able to relate to. It gives readers the opportunity to be made aware of how everyday language, both spoken and written, can be confusing and ambiguous, and how this can affect a person trying to navigate the world, but that the right environment can allow a person to thrive.'

— Robyn Steward, Autism Trainer, Mentor, Consultant and author of The Independent Woman's Handbook for Super Safe Living on the Autistic Spectrum

'I found *A Different Kettle of Fish* to be a thoroughly entertaining book, indeed I was chuckling out loud at times. It reflects a day in Michael's life and his interpretation of standard phrases that we take for granted but which take on a strange and comical literal meaning for a person on the autism spectrum. I have a son on the autism spectrum and so I can empathise with many of the points that Michael makes as Michael (this is my son Michael not the author!) starts arbitrarily telling me everything there is to know about his latest favourite plane. "Michael, you are driving me up the wall!" I say receiving a response, "Dad, how can you do that? You'll hit the ceiling!" This is a comforting read for all of us who have sat at traffic lights at road works looking at the sign "Heavy Plant Crossing" and waiting for the oak tree to lumber across the road. Perhaps there is a little autism in all of us.'

— Dr D. Faux, Senior Physics Lecturer, University of Surrey

'As a parent I feel so much better having read this book. My biggest worry has always been what the future will hold for my son, but I can now see a light at the end of the tunnel. An inspiration for teenagers with Asperger's or high-functioning autism.'

— Parent of a fourteen-year-old boy with autism

'I love Michael's amusing, yet reflective, illustrated account of a day in his shoes. Michael is sitting on the fence between the neurotypical and autistic worlds and acts as an interpreter to tell us what it's like on the other side. He has shown that with skill, focus and determination we can overcome the difficulties we face in life and is an example to us all. This book deserves a prominent place in every staffroom and classroom.'

— Christine Reveley, Inclusion Manager (SENCo)
at a mainstream primary school

'Absolutely bursting with little gems and insights. Michael gives the reader a very clear account of what life is really like for someone on the autism spectrum. What stands out is his ability to use easy-to-understand examples of how he thinks and sees the world. Essential reading for anyone involved with autism.'

— Sally Casey, Occupational Therapist,
Kent Community Health NHS Trust

'As a fan of Michael's first book on idioms, I was very pleased to read his latest work. In this new book, we accompany Michael, as he journeys through a typical day in his university life. It is simply delightful; as interesting and informative as it is amusing. The content will make it a huge hit with most children on the spectrum, but for me, as the mother of a young man with ASD, it is the glimpse of Michael's successful life that makes it so compelling. From judo to guitar playing to student status, Michael is truly cool and my only beef with this excellent book is that it came to an end far too quickly!'

— K.I. Al-Ghani, Special Education Teacher and Trainer,
and author of The Red Beast *and several books relating*
to special education for children and adults

'I loved Michael's book *It's Raining Cats and Dogs* and now this book gives us further insight into the complexities of our use of language and how it is assumed we understand the illogicality of ambiguous expressions. The book describes Michael's journey through a day out in London with all the pitfalls of potential miscommunication. The book is witty and fun to read and captures Michael's very positive outlook on life.'

— Dr Judith Gould, Director, The NAS Lorna Wing Centre for Autism

'Michael Barton has – once again – produced a beautiful and funny book, with his own fresh perspective on the bizarre idioms of the English language, rendering them more comprehensible to people on the autism spectrum. His attractive illustrations break up the text and the result is a gem of a slim book.'

— Professor Simon Baron-Cohen, Director of the Autism Research Centre, University of Cambridge

by the same author

It's Raining Cats and Dogs
An Autism Spectrum Guide to the Confusing World
of Idioms, Metaphors and Everyday Expressions
ISBN 978 1 84905 283 2
eISBN 978 0 85700 588 5

A DIFFERENT KETTLE OF FISH

A Day in the Life of a Physics Student with Autism

WRITTEN AND ILLUSTRATED BY
MICHAEL BARTON

Foreword by Delia Barton

Jessica Kingsley *Publishers*
London and Philadelphia

First published in 2014
by Jessica Kingsley Publishers
73 Collier Street
London N1 9BE, UK
and
400 Market Street, Suite 400
Philadelphia, PA 19106, USA

www.jkp.com

Copyright © Michael Barton 2014
Illustrations copyright © Michael Barton 2014
Foreword copyright © Delia Barton 2014

All rights reserved. No part of this publication may be reproduced in any
material form (including photocopying or storing it in any medium by electronic
means and whether or not transiently or incidentally to some other use of this
publication) without the written permission of the copyright owner except in
accordance with the provisions of the Copyright, Designs and Patents Act 1988
or under the terms of a licence issued by the Copyright Licensing Agency Ltd,
Saffron House, 6–10 Kirby Street, London EC1N 8TS. Applications for the
copyright owner's written permission to reproduce any part of this publication
should be addressed to the publisher.

Warning: The doing of an unauthorised act in relation to a copyright work may
result in both a civil claim for damages and criminal prosecution.

Library of Congress Cataloging in Publication Data
Barton, Michael, author.
  A different kettle of fish : a day in the life of a physics student with autism /
Michael Barton ; foreword
by Delia Barton ; illustrated by Michael Barton.
     pages cm
   ISBN 978-1-84905-532-1 (alk. paper)
  1. Barton, Michael--Health. 2. Autistic people--Language. 3. Autistic people--
Psychology. 4. London
(England) I. Title. II. Title: Day in the life of a physics student with autism.
   RC553.A88B3728 2014
   616.85'8832--dc23
                              2013048202

British Library Cataloguing in Publication Data
A CIP catalogue record for this book is available from the British Library

ISBN 978 1 84905 532 1
eISBN 978 0 85700 956 2

Printed and bound in Great Britain

CONTENTS

Foreword by Delia Barton 9

Introduction. 13

1 Journey into the Unknown. 17

2 Would Alan Turing Have Passed
   the Turing Test?. 31

3 How Long Would a Jumbo Jet Take
   to Get to Pluto?. 39

4 Payment by Chicken. 45

5 Assorted Pig Organs. 53

6 The World is Your Lobster 61

7 Back in a Familiar World 69

Afterword 75

Glossary of Idioms 77

FOREWORD

Reading this book will be both informative and entertaining for anyone who has anything to do with autism. Michael has an endearingly upbeat attitude towards his autism, as well as a positive outlook on life. People with autism often describe their autism as a different way of being; hence the title of the book, *A Different Kettle of Fish*. I can just imagine Michael saying, 'What has a kettle full of fish got to do with anything?'

More and more children and adults are being diagnosed with autism. Understanding how they think is the key to supporting them and helping them develop in such a way that allows them to realise their full potential.

Michael is a student with high-functioning autism, currently studying physics at university, who appears to be able to act as an interpreter between the autistic world and the rest of us by showing us, with examples and drawings, how his mind operates on a day-to-day basis.

In this book he describes a day trip from the comfort of his familiar environment on the university campus to the hustle and bustle of central London. Michael's depiction of his logical world makes one realise just how incomprehensible we must be to people with autism.

His examples of the confusion that indirect questions can cause are truly eye-opening. For instance, when I was on the phone once and the doorbell rang I called to Michael, 'I'm on the phone!' He had absolutely no idea that I really meant, 'Please will you answer the door?'

Fortunately, he views much of our illogical world as comedic and positively enjoys the ridiculous idioms and signs he sees, much in the same way as we enjoy nonsense rhymes or Pythonesque humour. A sign in a shop window that says, 'Guide dogs only' elicits the thought, 'Well, they're not going to do much business if *people* aren't allowed in there!' Sayings like, 'No need to bite my head off!' conjure up bizarre images, and when someone says, 'I'd have to break a leg to get to my meeting on time' he feels quite concerned that the person might actually break his own leg, and thinks, 'How is he going to walk to his meeting with an injury like that?'

Michael also describes how he has learnt to use his skills to overcome some of the difficulties he experiences, in particular how his music and membership of judo and rock climbing clubs has enabled him to socialise and make friends.

One of the hardest things for us to understand about autism is the fact that it covers such a wide range of abilities, from those needing 24-hour care on the one hand, to industry leaders and scientists on the other. In addition, each individual can display a remarkably uneven profile. They can be experts in certain areas, yet be totally clueless about simple everyday things that we just take for granted.

It transpires that, usually, we are to blame for the confusion they encounter. If only we could see the world as they do and speak plainly, explain what is expected of them and be as honest and straightforward as they are, the majority of their problems would not exist. I firmly believe that it is up to us to step into their world instead of always expecting them to conform to ours.

We need to learn from people like Michael, be tolerant of their differences and embrace their skills. They clearly have a place in modern society, and without them the world would be very different.

Delia Barton

INTRODUCTION

Throughout this book I shall be describing a day in which I travel from university, in Guildford, to London and back. This book is very much written in terms of how I think of things.

Autism is referred to as a spectrum condition because it affects different people in different ways. At one end of the spectrum you have people who are quite severely affected by autism, referred to as those with low-functioning autism. These individuals may be non-verbal and may require support in their daily routines throughout their lives. At the other end of the spectrum you may find it hard to tell that the person is on the spectrum at all. Therefore, I assume that not everybody on the spectrum will interpret things the same way that I do. However, numerous points mentioned in this book will apply to many other people with autism.

As I have grown older I have learnt to adapt to the world around me and, as a result, I am able to provide a peep through the keyhole into the world of autism. One of the most prominent traits people with autism display is difficulty communicating well with others. My book aims to show you what the world is like for me as an 'autist'.

The terminology used in the autism community varies. Some like to be referred to as 'autistic people', others think the politically correct term is 'a person with autism' or even 'someone on the autistic spectrum'. Asperger's syndrome is sometimes used for those on the high-functioning end of the spectrum, a diagnosis not given to me because I started talking late. I personally prefer being referred to as an autist. I believe that all terms are equally acceptable.

I have decided to use the word 'neurotypical' – short for 'neurologically typical' – to describe somebody not on the autistic spectrum. I also occasionally refer to neurotypicals as 'ordinary' people as they represent the vast majority of the population. Please don't take offence when I use the word ordinary – I just can't think of a better word.

'Autistic traits', another term that I like to use, are characteristics common to people anywhere on the autistic spectrum. However, they're not exclusively displayed by those on the autistic spectrum. Many scientists and mathematicians show some of these traits – for example, being very logical and methodical in their thinking. Most neurotypical people prefer things to be scheduled and like knowing what's going to happen next, albeit maybe not to the same extent as autistic people. Therefore, I feel that instead of imagining that there are separate autistic and neurotypical spectrums, it's better to think of a 'human' spectrum as there is no concrete borderline between the two (or a borderline made out of any material!).

In other words, we're all different.

Michael Barton

1

JOURNEY INTO
THE UNKNOWN

'Didn't you smell a rat?'

My radio alarm has just woken me up and a director of one of the major banks is being interviewed about the latest banking scandal.

What on earth does smelling a rat have to do with banking? It seems to make perfect sense to the interviewer, yet I have absolutely no idea what he's talking about!

A mental image of a smelly rat comes to mind.

TO SMELL A RAT

I know that dead rats smell, but even if you were to find a rat in a bank I'm sure it wouldn't make headline news! It must therefore just be an expression, so I have to figure out what it really means. I conclude that it probably means that they have done something wrong and they should have 'smelled the rat', or recognised the problem, earlier.

Or, as described later in the interview, they had egg on their face.

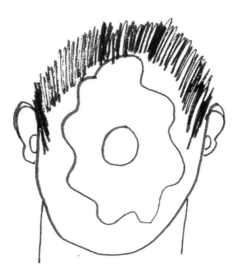

HE HAD EGG ON HIS FACE

I'm a physics student at university living on campus with 12 other students on my floor. I've always liked physics because there's a lot of problem solving and it means that I can apply my mathematical expertise to real-life situations.

I walk into the kitchen to make a cup of tea and meet one of the other students.

'Morning, Michael. Great news about the Higgs boson, isn't it?'

'Brilliant', I say. 'I've already heard a joke about it. A Higgs boson walks into a church and says, "Hold on. You can't have mass without me!"' We both crack up laughing and then spend the next five minutes discussing various aspects of the newly discovered particle and the impact it might have on our understanding of particle physics. This is one of the great things about being at a science university – everyone I speak to here is on the same wavelength as me (pun intended!) and I can start a conversation with almost anyone.

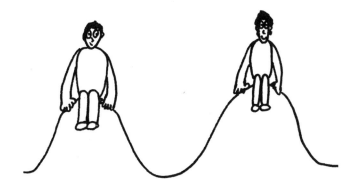

PEOPLE ON THE SAME WAVELENGTH

I'm off to the Alan Turing exhibition at the Science Museum today because I'm interested in exploring the links between great mathematical brains and autism.

Alan Turing must be one of the most famous mathematicians of all time so I'm really looking forward to finding out more about his inventions and work. He made the fundamental theoretical breakthrough that led to the development of the modern-day computer and was possibly our most important codebreaker in the Second World War (more on him later). It has been suggested that he was on the autistic spectrum owing to his exceptionally strong analytical, mathematical and problem-solving skills, which, when combined with stories of communication and social difficulties, certainly point to that conclusion.

Einstein is another scientist that people believe had autistic traits. He was once asked why he was a genius, and replied, 'I don't think I am a genius; I just stick at things longer than most people.'

Stephen Hawking once said, 'Sometimes it is years before I see the way forward. In the case of information loss and black holes, it was 29 years.'

There's no suggestion that Stephen Hawking is autistic, but, as with Einstein, the ability to stay focused for long periods of time is certainly an autistic trait, and I see it as a common theme among great scientists and mathematicians.

I leave the comfort and familiarity of the university campus and set off to walk down to the station. After a few minutes, I pass a couple of ladies pushing a pram containing a particularly plump baby. As I walk past I overhear the first lady saying, '...and he made it by the skin of his teeth.'

HE MADE IT BY THE SKIN OF HIS TEETH

'That'll teach him to stick his neck out,' says the second lady.

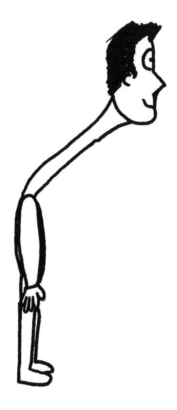

HE STUCK HIS NECK OUT

'Well he's not out of the woods yet. He's just got too much on his plate at the moment.'

What on earth are they talking about? As far as I am concerned they might as well be speaking Japanese!

NOT OUT OF THE WOODS BECAUSE HE HAS TOO MUCH ON HIS PLATE

At the station I buy a ticket at the machine and find the correct platform. I'm waiting patiently for the train when an announcement comes over the Tannoy system: 'This is an announcement.' My immediate thought is, 'Of course it's an announcement, what else would it be?' The voice continues: 'For your safety, passengers must remain behind the yellow line at all times.' This makes me smile every time I hear it because I know I have to cross the yellow line in order to get on my train!

I look up at the display to see if the train is on time but it says:

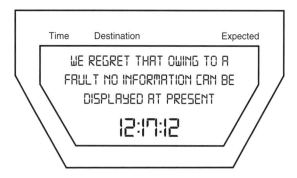

It is telling me that no information can be displayed, which is clearly not true! Plus it also displays the time, which I think is useful information to know.

Thirteen minutes later I'm still waiting, so I begin to get annoyed because there have been no announcements about the delay. The train was due to arrive at the platform for a 12:20 departure but it's now 12:30. This wouldn't have been so bad if they had told me that the train would be delayed by ten minutes, but not knowing how late the train is going to be is irritating as I always like to be precise with my time. The train arrives at 12:33, 13 minutes late (grrr!), and we depart at 12:35.

I step over the yellow line (hoping that nobody will catch me!) and board the train. It's not very busy so I find myself a seat by the window and make myself comfortable. I'm looking out of the window listening to my iPod when the passenger sitting opposite me asks me if this is the right train to go to London Waterloo.

I answer, 'Yeah.'

He then starts talking about the train being late and says, 'I'd have to break a leg to get to my meeting on time if this train is delayed any further!'

TO BREAK A LEG

I feel quite concerned about him breaking his own leg, and think, 'How is he going to walk to his meeting with an injury like that?' I then realise that he probably won't do this (that's a stupid thing for anyone to do!) and that he must mean something else, but what? I'm not really sure.

He then asks me a couple of other questions, to which I give short, abrupt answers. I've always been told not to speak with strangers and I really don't like it when people I don't know start talking to me on a train.

I'm fine with talking to new people after having given a talk at a conference or meeting, or at a party, for example, because these are situations where you would expect to be talking to people you've never met before.

As soon as he stops talking I pick up a discarded newspaper that someone's left on the seat next to me. Most of it is mind-numbingly boring, so I glance through it quickly, trying to find something interesting. There are no articles about science so I start scanning the text looking for interesting idioms and come across a sentence that says, 'People should stop *throwing white elephants and red herrings* at each other.' I haven't a clue what this means, but I like the image it conjures up.

THROWING WHITE ELEPHANTS AND RED HERRINGS AT EACH OTHER

The train eventually arrives at London Waterloo and I make my way down to the underground. The tube train comes in and I see that most of the seats are taken, so I find somewhere to stand. When we arrive at my stop an announcement says, 'Please let other people off the train first.' I think to myself, 'If everybody obeyed this instruction, nobody could get off the train!' As other people leave the train I do as well, thereby obeying this rule to some extent. (I couldn't have let *everybody* else off before me because some people wouldn't be getting off at this stop.)

Upon reaching the escalator I read a sign at the bottom saying a few things, one of which is 'Dogs must be carried.'

A picture of a man carrying a large dog appears in my mind:

DOGS MUST BE CARRIED

I smile at the ridiculousness of it and then think, 'I don't have a dog, so how am I supposed to use this escalator?' But then I see that nobody on the escalator is carrying a dog, so I step on, hoping that I too can get away with not carrying one.

When I leave the station I walk up the road to the Science Museum and pass another sign about dogs, but this time it's on a bin and says, 'Please be a responsible dog owner.'

My first thought is 'What if I don't want a dog?' My second thought is 'If I did decide to follow the instructions on the sign, where on earth would I get a responsible dog?'

If that wasn't enough to make me get a dog, I then pass a newsagents bearing the sign:

Guide dogs only

They're not going to do much business if *people* aren't allowed in there!

So now I've figured out that I need to get a dog in order to use the escalators on the underground, be a responsible dog owner and go into newsagents.

2

WOULD ALAN TURING HAVE PASSED THE TURING TEST?

I arrive at the Science Museum. There's no charge at the gate, they just ask for a donation. As I'm a student and not made of money (the human body is mainly water) I put a £1 coin in the box and proceed straight to the Alan Turing exhibition.

HE'S MADE OF MONEY

The exhibition is entitled 'Codebreaker' because Turing is mainly known for his work during the Second World War, when he ran a team that deciphered the secret codes that the German military used to encrypt sensitive messages.

One of his other main achievements was inventing the Automatic Computing Engine (ACE), an early computer, which was on display. It's interesting that we think of computers as electronic devices, yet computers were originally people who computed – in other words, people, mainly women at the time, who worked on machines performing repetitive calculations.

A COMPUTER

I was also reminded about the Turing test – a test of artificial intelligence, which computers would pass if they appeared indistinguishable from people. The test involves someone asking questions of the computer – if they can't tell whether it is the computer or an actual person providing the answers the computer is said to have passed the test (i.e. it is displaying intelligent behaviour). So far we've only invented computers that can pass the Turing test at the intelligence level of a five-year-old child.

I think one reason he came up with the Turing test was because he wanted to break down the way that *he* thought into computer terms. People with high-functioning autism think very logically and analytically (similar to how computers operate) compared to ordinary people. Therefore, perhaps Alan Turing was looking for a way to systemise how he thought, and his research into artificial intelligence was his way of trying to map it out. If he was autistic, as suspected, he may have simply been expressing how he himself, as a 'logical computer', thought and communicated.

I wonder if Alan Turing himself would have passed the Turing test? If the test were to be performed on an ordinary person and an autistic person, I think many of the questions would elicit answers that might lead the tester to conclude that the autistic person was a computer.

The way I think when I hear a new idiom can be expressed as a simple flow chart. Consider 'It's raining cats and dogs' (the title of my last book).

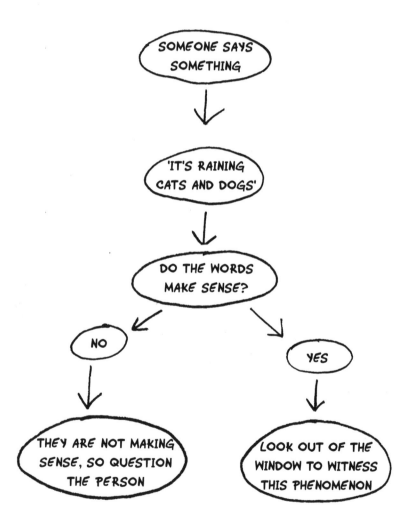

This could be described by a computer program which translates computer code into a 'high-level language' that the man in the street can understand.

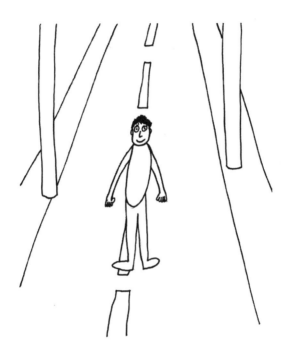

THE MAN IN THE STREET

It seems to me that neurotypical people's thinking might be described by a massive 'spider diagram' (a diagram that looks like a spider's web, with multiple concepts joined to each other by logical connections). So when they hear idioms, neurotypical people have interconnecting links that say, 'They don't actually mean this, they mean something else.'

I asked my dad what his thought process might be when he hears a new idiom like 'It's raining cats and dogs.' He said that he hears the expression and then subconsciously thinks about numerous possible interpretations, and for each he considers whether it's sensible, whether it's reasonable, whether it's likely and whether or not it might be humour. He then reaches a consensus and concludes that it means it's raining hard.

Autistic people, like myself, only consider what's actually been said, so we assume that the idiom is logically correct, which is where the confusion arises, sending autistic people on a wild goose chase.

GOING ON A WILD GOOSE CHASE

So maybe it was this alternative way of thinking that proved beneficial for Alan Turing, as it let him think outside the box (autistic people tend not to be able to see any box, or boundaries, and so are sometimes able to see a problem and imagine a solution that does not rely on what has gone before).

THINKING OUTSIDE THE BOX

Many people at the high-functioning end of the autistic spectrum are labelled as having Asperger's syndrome, which named after Hans Asperger, who first documented the condition. He called children with Asperger's 'little professors' because of their ability to talk about their favourite subject in great detail. Asperger noticed that many of the children he identified as being autistic utilised their special talents in adulthood and had successful careers.

He said, 'I am convinced that autistic people have their place in the organism of the social community. They fulfil their role well, perhaps better than anyone else could, and we are talking of people who as children had the greatest difficulties and caused untold worries to their care-givers.'

Everything I've found out today about Alan Turing suggests to me that he did indeed have high-functioning autism or Asperger's. Certainly, the contributions he made towards cracking the German wartime codes were immense. It is said that he and his team probably reduced the duration of the war by at least six months. If that isn't a major contribution to society, then I don't know what is.

3

HOW LONG WOULD A JUMBO JET TAKE TO GET TO PLUTO?

I leave the Alan Turing exhibition, fascinated by all that he has done, and wander round the rest of the Science Museum. There are lots of school children about and it takes me back to my school days (I don't mean literally – no time machines involved, unfortunately!).

I was always good at science and maths at school because of my memory for facts and logical way of thinking. Subjects like English and religious studies are based more upon getting your opinion across in an elaborate way rather than learning the facts, and so are a different kettle of fish.

A DIFFERENT KETTLE OF FISH

Of course I mean that they are completely different types of subjects.

I really struggled with my English GCSE and remember an exam question asking me to 'Discuss the humour in this passage.' I didn't find it funny, so I wrote 'There isn't any.' In my opinion that was the right answer but I now know I had been expected to write a five-page essay on why other people might find it funny.

I reach the solar system exhibit at the Science Museum. I remember being extremely interested in space when I was a kid and used to find out all I could about it. I was extremely passionate about the subject and would talk about it incessantly, telling anyone that would listen things like 'Do you know how long it would take to travel to Pluto in a jumbo jet? Well, the Earth is 2.67 billion miles away so a jumbo jet travelling at 567mph would take 538 years to get to Pluto.'

JUMBO JET FLYING TO PLUTO

You often find autistic kids memorising interesting facts like this. They can recall them on demand, but also have a tendency to talk about them whenever they feel like it (irrelevant to the current conversation topic!).

I'm looking at the solar system display when I hear a child close by shouting at his mum, to which she replies, 'No need to bite my head off!'

I've heard of laughing your head off (to laugh a lot) and even biting your tongue (to be quiet), but biting someone's head off puts a rather more vivid picture into my mind!

BITING SOMEONE'S HEAD OFF

Why can't people just say what they mean instead of making it this complicated? I just can't get my head around it!

GET YOUR HEAD AROUND IT

New Scientist magazine published an interview
with me on the topic of the English language. It
was entitled 'Going Bananas, Laughing Your Head
Off. English is a minefield if you have autism, says
the student aiming to decode it.' I was asked why
autistic people find the English language so confusing,
to which I replied, 'Autistic people think in black
and white and therefore interpret everything
very literally. Ordinary people seem to love using
idioms, metaphors and figurative speech, whether
to aid communication or simply to make life more
interesting, whereas for autistic people they simply
make no sense.'

I've seen all I want at the Science Museum so
I venture out onto the streets of London. I go in a

mini-supermarket to buy a drink and hear a young child screaming and shouting in the shop. A few people have gathered around and are looking at the mother trying to calm her child, who seems to be having a meltdown. I wonder what's upset the child. It's a very busy shop with lots of people wandering around and gossiping, flickering, fluorescent lights and a machine buzzing and whirring in an unusual way. I find these noises disturbing, so it occurs to me that the child might be autistic and just can't bear the environment. I hear one onlooker say, 'What a spoilt child. Her mother should teach her how to behave.' If only the general public were more aware of autism and the difficulties people with autism face. In my opinion, people who say things like this are displaying the following characteristics:

- a lack of empathy

- poor communication skills

- a dislike of difference or change

- rigidity in their thinking.

I find it ironic that these are some of the traits that autistic people tend to display!

4

PAYMENT BY CHICKEN

Having left the Science Museum I decide to walk over to Denmark Street to look in the music shops for a new guitar strap. It's a good 40-minute walk, but I'm fit and I like walking around London as I regularly see high performance cars on the road, which I have been interested in ever since my dad bought me a *What Car?* magazine when I was ten.

I was an expert on the Pokémon card game at the time and knew every single detail about every single card, which impressed people at school but infuriated my dad as I'd sometimes talk non-stop about different aspects of the game. As he knew nothing about Pokémon (nor was he interested, unfortunately for me), he thought that getting me interested in cars instead would give me something to talk about with him, without him getting bored to tears.

DAD GETTING BORED TO TEARS

When I got the *What Car?* magazine I read it from cover to cover and memorised every detail about every car in the magazine, becoming particularly keen on the most powerful cars. I would then talk about cars at every available opportunity, which was most of the time, and Dad was happy to listen to me for a few days…until he got bored again and bought me a book on astronomy!

I spot an Aston Martin DBS and instantly reel off its vital statistics in my head: 5.9 litre V12 engine producing 510hp and a 0–62mph time of 4.3 seconds, achieving a top speed of 191mph. Brilliant!

THE ASTON MARTIN DBS

I arrive at Denmark Street and pop into a music shop.

POPPING INTO A SHOP

I take a look around and admire the guitars on show. Someone is trying out a guitar but needs to put a bit more practice in (in my opinion!).

Music is an important part of my life. I've spent thousands of hours practising music, having begun a strict daily practice schedule at age eight and practising almost every day since. I think music is a universal language – one that everyone can understand in some form or another. I have played in numerous bands and made friends because of my musical abilities. In my opinion it's important to make the most of what you're good at.

I find a strap that I like and pay at the till. The cashier says, 'How are you going to pay?' I think to myself, 'Isn't that an obvious question? With money, of course – I'm not exactly going to give her a chicken, am I?!'

PAYING BY CHICKEN

I reply 'What do you mean?'

'Cash or card?' is her reply.

I hand her the appropriate cash, get my change, then walk out of the shop with my new strap.

Central London is known for being busy, which means there is lots of background noise that I find unsettling; however, I have been to London often enough to be able to tolerate it. My way of coping is to pay more attention to my immediate surroundings to help cancel out the background noise. This works because when autistic people focus, they REALLY focus. However, they aren't as good at focusing when a number of things are going on simultaneously as they find it difficult to know which thing to prioritise. Hence, they can easily get distracted by things that neurotypical people simply ignore.

I make my way to Covent Garden because I like to see all the different performers busking. A skiffle band there catches my eye. (Skiffle is a type of popular music usually made using homemade or improvised instruments.)

CATCHING MY EYE

This reminds me of the time I went on a rock climbing holiday in Cornwall (I've been a member of the Rock Climbing Club since I started at uni). One night we went to a pub and there was a skiffle band playing. The band leader was playing something that looked halfway between a banjo and a ukulele, so I went up to him in the interval to ask him about it. He told me it was a banjulele, a cross between a banjo and a ukulele (I was right!). I mentioned that I play the spoons, and he was very keen on this and invited me to play a couple of numbers with them in the second half, which I did. It totally amazed all of my rock climbing friends, none of whom knew that I was a musician, let alone a virtuoso spoons player! (I have to confess here that I was taught how to play by probably the best spoons player in the world, the hugely talented and famous Sam Spoons of the legendary Bonzo Dog Doo Dah Band.) I was very pleased when one of them said to me afterwards, 'Wow. You really are the Jimi Hendrix of spoons, aren't you?!'

ME PLAYING THE SPOONS

5

ASSORTED PIG ORGANS

I'm getting hungry so I think about lunch. Do I feel like a kebab?

I FEEL LIKE A KEBAB

Or some chips? I know – I feel like a Chinese!

I FEEL LIKE A CHINESE

I head over to Chinatown. When I get there the Chinese people outnumber everyone else so it feels like I'm a foreigner, even though I'm in London!

I know what it feels like to be in a foreign country because I went on exchange visits to France, Germany and Spain when I was at school. I'm good at learning languages because of my memory for facts, so it has always been easy for me to quickly develop a large vocabulary. Being a foreigner in France, for example, was actually a huge advantage for me because the French didn't expect me to understand idioms and figures of speech in their language and they would always speak to me as clearly as possible and say exactly what they meant. Also, if I was rather blunt or tactless in my responses they would put it down to my imperfect language skills rather than my autism (if only everyone could do this all the time!).

I choose a restaurant that I've been to with my family before, so I know it's going to be good. Looking at the menu I see that the translations aren't quite perfect. Assorted pig organs are on the menu, which I have tried before when my dad, being adventurous, actually ordered them!

I remember attending a social skills group once and they said they wanted to ask us all a few questions first to 'break the ice'.

BREAKING THE ICE

One question was 'What's the most unusual food you've eaten before?' and I think my response of 'assorted pig organs' was the best!

The ducks' tongues and chicken feet don't sound too appealing. Pigs' ears are also on the menu and I've heard that they are quite a delicacy in China. Pig's ear is cockney rhyming slang for beer, so I wonder whether I should order a few!

Cockney rhyming slang (s.lang = secret language) was developed so that it could only be understood by those who spoke it. For example, does 'I grabbed my mushy peas and popped out in the jam jar to go for a kitchen sink' make any sense to you? It's just like the idioms people use every day that totally confuse foreigners (and autistic people).

GOING OUT IN THE JAM JAR FOR A KITCHEN SINK

In simple, understandable English this all means 'I grabbed my keys and popped out in the car to go for a drink.'

A brilliant example of unintelligible cockney I heard was on an old radio programme called *Hancock's Half Hour*, which my dad loves. One of the characters says, 'Marvellous, isn't it? I can't wait to get into my pointed Italian two tones and off down the

High Street. Makes you feel like a king. Clean dicky dirt, new Peckham, pair of luminous almond rocks, new whistle, nice crease in my strides, Barnet well greased up and flashing my Hampsteads at all the bona palones.'

THE MAN DESCRIBED ABOVE

If you are a neurotypical, and non-cockney, person reading this, you now have an idea of what it's like for autistic people when they hear idioms!

By the way, as far as I can work out, this bizarre sentence is a mixture of cockney rhyming slang and another slang, which is used in London, called Polari slang.

Dicky dirt   shirt

Peckham (Rye)   tie

almond rocks   socks

whistle (and flute)   suit

strides (Australian slang)   trousers

Barnet (Fair)   hair

Hampstead (Heath)   teeth

bona palones (Polari slang)   nice girls

THE WORLD IS
YOUR LOBSTER

I decide to hop onto a bus (not literally, of course, but an entertaining mental image of a queue of people taking it in turns to 'hop on' appears) back to London Waterloo.

HOPPING ONTO THE BUS

I find a seat upstairs and enjoy the views as we head to the station. When we arrive I disobey the sign that says:

PASSENGERS MUST REMAIN
SEATED AT ALL TIMES

I walk into Waterloo station to find that I've just missed a train, so I have to wait for 20 minutes. I pop into the newsagents (there was no sign saying 'Guide dogs only') and buy the latest edition of *New Scientist* and the satirical magazine *Private Eye*.

I always like reading the 'Commentatorballs' section in *Private Eye* because it gives great examples of commentators saying ridiculous things. My favourite one was during Wimbledon when the commentator said 'Andy Murray was forcing Federer to make unforced errors.' They also often have great examples of malapropisms (also known as 'phonological word substitutions'). As if idioms aren't hard enough for autistic people to understand, a malapropism is when people say the wrong word in an idiom or expression! I once heard someone say, 'The world is your lobster!'

THE WORLD IS YOUR LOBSTER

They actually meant to say 'The world is your oyster' (equally ridiculous in my opinion). The thing I find remarkable is that ordinary people seem to understand what is being talked about, despite the wrong words being used.

I've still got 15 minutes to wait until my train leaves, so I sit down on one of the benches on the platform and flick through my *New Scientist* magazine. An article that discusses work on a cure (or 'treatment', as they call it) for autism catches my eye. I find this rather disturbing as it is obvious to me that evolution would have weeded out autism a long time ago unless there was some overall advantage to our species. I'm all for finding ways to help those people who are severely affected by autism, but there are undoubtedly many people with autism who are making fantastic contributions to the world. Apart from all that, I have high-functioning autism, and I'm very happy with my life. I am thus rather alarmed when I hear talk of a 'cure' or 'treatment'. It's just totally illogical!

My train arrives at the platform and I'm yet again forced to cross the yellow line in order to board. I find a window seat and relax, knowing I'm heading back to uni. The train departs and a few minutes later the ticket inspector walks down the aisle.

He asks me, 'Do you have a ticket?' I immediately think, 'Yes, I do have a ticket', then work out that he wants to see it. So I show him my valid ticket and he carries on his way down the train.

Indirect requests like this have caused me quite a lot of problems in the past. As with idioms, my brain processes the request literally (i.e. logically). So if I didn't realise that a question was an indirect request, I would answer directly. For example, if someone asked, 'Can you pass me the salt?' my immediate thought was 'Of course I can' (I have the ability to pass them the salt), so I would reply 'Yes' but not actually pass it to them!

CAN YOU PASS ME THE SALT?

However, I've now learnt that if someone asks me a question like this they really means, 'Please will you pass me the salt?' and therefore I do so. As I've got older I think my brain logic has developed a new link that says to me, 'If someone says something that doesn't make any sense at all, they probably mean something else.' So when I hear new idioms or indirect questions now, although my initial reaction is to process the information literally, a second process follows almost immediately that helps me to think of the true meaning.

But I still struggle occasionally. Some indirect requests seem to me to have absolutely no resemblance to what the person really wants. For example, when my mum was on the phone recently, the doorbell rang and she called out to me, 'I'm on the phone!' What does being on the phone have to do with the doorbell? In fact she meant, 'Please will you answer the door for me?'

I watch the stations fly by on my way back to Guildford.

THE STATIONS FLYING BY

When we get to the station I get off the train and as I reach the exit I notice a ticket inspector arguing with a teenage boy.

'Look, it's very simple. If you can't produce a ticket you have to pay the fine.'

'But I've lost it!' shouted the boy.

'You can shout at me until the cows come home,' said the inspector, 'but it won't do you any good. You're just going to have to take it on the chin and pay the fine.'

I'm feeling rather tired after my day in London, so I can't be bothered to try and work out how cows and chins could possibly have anything to do with losing a ticket.

COWS COMING HOME AND SOMEONE
TAKING IT ON THE CHIN

7

BACK IN A
FAMILIAR WORLD

I walk back to my room on campus and pass one of my fellow physics students on the way.

'Hi Mikey', he says cheerfully. 'Did you manage to work out how to do that quantum mechanics question we were set the other day?'

'Oh yes', I replied. 'Piece of cake in the end.'

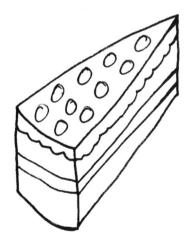

A PIECE OF CAKE

I feel more at ease now that I'm back in familiar surroundings because I know the campus really well and the people I meet talk normally (i.e. without using bizarre idioms and metaphors!). But as soon as I think that, I realise that I've just used one myself and start wondering exactly where the expression 'a piece of cake' came from. So it's not that I don't use idioms myself, it's just that I need to learn each one individually, whereas ordinary people seem to instinctively know what they mean the first time they hear them.

I've enjoyed my day out, but it's good to be back.

I'd made sure I was back in time for Judo in the evening. I founded the University of Surrey Judo Club in my first year. It has now developed into a successful club with around 20 regular members, frequent social events and the higher grades taking part in national judo competitions. Judo is great because the instructions given are always really clear and precise (and usually repeated), plus the discipline means that the strict rules are always adhered to. On top of all this it's a great competitive sport, and a great feeling when you throw someone!

ME THROWING SOMEONE IN JUDO

I started doing judo when I was eight years old and would recommend it to anyone, because it stops you from getting bullied at school (a very common problem for children who are different) and gives you a huge amount of self-confidence. Also, as I got better, I found that some of the other boys would like to hang out with me so they wouldn't get bullied either.

Since being at university I've actually found it quite easy to make friends. I think this is because I'm with like-minded people, and because when you start at university you're all in the same boat!

ALL IN THE SAME BOAT

The whole atmosphere at university is generally very friendly. Particularly in Freshers' Week, when you sign up to join clubs, as the students want lots of people to join to make it a successful club. I've made most of my friends via clubs because you're with people who have a similar interest. This friendly atmosphere and wide variety of clubs and events has made university the best years of my life (so far)!

On a final note:

Something my dad told me many times from an early age is that life is like a card game. If we're dealt a hand with lots of low cards, we still play it to the best of our ability, because sometimes we still win, despite the poor hand. Some people are born with lots of high cards – for example, they have good social skills, are good at sports, good at music, etc. – and some people have a bunch of low cards – perhaps they have a disability, or are not good at something. In this situation you've got two choices. You can either go away and cry about it and feel sorry for yourself, or accept it and play the cards to the best of your ability. I've got some high cards – for example, my logical brain and intense focus make me good at music and maths. However, I'm working on my low cards – writing this book is helping my English, and playing music and doing judo and rock climbing puts me into social situations where people are keen to talk to me because of my skills.

So the moral of the story is, play the hand you're dealt with and stop wishing for a different one.

THE HAND OF CARDS YOU'RE DEALT WITH

AFTERWORD

Everything I've learnt about autism suggests to me that autistic people definitely have their place in society. Steve Jobs, who founded Apple Computers, summed it up nicely when he said:

> 'Here's to the crazy ones. The misfits. The rebels. The troublemakers. The round pegs in the square holes. The ones who see things differently... They have no respect for the status quo. You can quote them, disagree with them, glorify or vilify them. About the only thing you can't do is ignore them. Because they change things. They push the human race forward.'

As the 21st century progresses, I can see the world moving into a new scientific era where the demand for autistic people's highly logical skills will increase exponentially. I feel we need to be thinking seriously about the impact we are having on the planet, which means paying more attention to what scientists are saying. In additon, as *Star Trek*'s Mr Spock said in one episode:

> '*Nowhere am I so desperately needed as among a shipload of illogical humans.*'

GLOSSARY OF IDIOMS

To smell a rat
To suspect that something is wrong, or that someone is being dishonest

He had egg on his face
He was embarrassed or humiliated by something he had done

People on the same wavelength
People who have similar thoughts on a topic

He made it by the skin of his teeth
He only just made it

He stuck his neck out
He took a risk

Not out of the woods
Still in danger or difficulty

To have too much on your plate
To be too busy to do anything else

To break a leg
To be very lucky

Throwing white elephants and red herrings at each other:
- A *white elephant* is an endeavour, venture or thing that proves to be useless
- A *red herring* is something that distracts you from the main issue
- Therefore, throwing white elephants and red herrings at each other means avoiding the main issue by distraction and irrelevancy

He's made of money
He has a lot of money

The man in the street
The ordinary, typical, average man

Going on a wild goose chase
Wasting your time on something you're not going to achieve

Thinking outside the box
Thinking in a different way

A different kettle of fish
A totally different matter

Biting someone's head off
To reply sharply or angrily to someone

I can't get my head around it
I just can't understand it

Bored to tears
Extremely bored

Pop into a shop
Briefly visit a shop

It catches my eye
It gets my attention

I feel like a kebab
I feel like eating a kebab

I feel like a Chinese
I feel like having some Chinese food

Breaking the ice
Doing something to help people feel more comfortable around each other (used mostly when people haven't met before)

Hopping onto a bus
Getting onto a bus

The world is your oyster
You have many opportunities ahead; you're in charge

Can you pass me the salt?
Pass me the salt please

The stations fly by
The stations go by quickly

Until the cows come home
For a very long time

You'll have to take it on the chin
You'll have to accept the consequences of your actions

It's a piece of cake
It's really easy

You're all in the same boat
You're all in the same situation

On a final note
A last few words I'd like to say